Jazz Piano Vocabulary

Volume 6
The Aeolian Mode

by Roberta Piket

With additional material available
on-line at www.muse-eek.com

Muse Eek Publishing Company
New York, New York

Copyright © 2007 by Roberta Piket. All rights reserved

ISBN 1594899606

No part of this publication may be reproduced, stored in a
retrieval system, or transmitted, in any form or by any means,
electronic, mechanical, photocopying, recording, or otherwise,
without the prior written permission of the publisher.

Printed in the United States

This publication can be purchased from your local bookstore or by contacting:
Muse Eek Publishing Company
P.O. Box 509
New York, NY 10276, USA
Phone: 212-473-7030
Fax: 212-473-4601
http://www.muse-eek.com
sales@muse-eek.com

Table of Contents

Acknowledgements	iv
About the Author	v
Foreword	vi
How to Use This Book	vii
Swung Eighth Notes	viii
Order of Presentation	viii
Fingering	ix
Introduction to the Aeolian Mode	10
Applying the Aeolian Mode to Improvisation	12
Left Hand Chords: "Shell" Voicings	18
Major ii-V-I Shell Voicings	19
Minor ii-V-i Shell Voicings	21
Aeolian Modes with Fingerings	23
Hand Position	23
Swung Eighth Notes, Articulation and Phrasing	23
The Modes	24
The Minor Blues Progression	28
Further Exploration	31

Acknowledgments

The author gratefully acknowledges Bruce Arnold for his invaluable feedback and Muse Eek Publishing for the opportunity to publish this book.

The author would also like to thank Mike Garson for permission to use his beautiful artwork.

Special thanks to Billy Mintz for everything.

About the Author

Roberta Piket is from Queens, NY. Her father, composer Frederick Piket, gave her her first piano lessons when she was seven years old. Roberta began playing seriously in her early teens, studying jazz piano with Walter Bishop, Jr and classical piano with Vera Wels. After graduating from prestigious Hunter College High School, she entered the joint double-degree program at Tufts University and the New England Conservatory of Music, earning a Bachelor's Degree in Computer Science from the former and a Bachelor's Degree in Jazz Studies from the latter. During this time she studied privately with Fred Hersch, Stanley Cowell, Jim McNeely and Bob Moses. Soon after graduation Roberta returned to New York City to devote herself to music full-time, which she has done ever since. In New York, she studied for six years with Richie Beirach and also studied briefly with Sofia Rosoff.

Roberta has performed professionally as a sidewoman with David Liebman, Rufus Reid, Michael Formanek, Lionel Hampton, Mickey Roker, Harvey Wainapel, Eliot Zigmund, Billy Mintz, and the BMI/New York Jazz Orchestra, and has twice been a featured guest on *Marian McPartland's Piano Jazz*, on National Public Radio.

Roberta has held master classes and/or clinics at the Eastman School of Music, California Institute of the Arts, Rutgers University, Duke University, as well as many other institutions in the U.S., Europe, and Japan.

Roberta has six CDs as a leader which have frequently made the jazz magazines' yearly top ten lists. In addition to freelancing on piano and organ, she currently leads her own piano trio. *Piano & Keyboard* recently called Roberta "one of the most accomplished and inventive young jazz pianists currently working on the scene."

More information about Roberta's music can be found at her web site: www.RobertaJazz.com.

Foreword

Many instrumentalists wish to pursue jazz improvisation, but are intimidated because they don't know what notes to play over chord changes, beyond the chord tones themselves. Frequently students are first instructed to use the blues scale to play over a blues, because it is an easy scale to learn and can be applied to a whole set of changes. Once they have mastered the blue scales many students do not know where to go next. This book provides an entry point for the student who wishes to start exploring the modes. Beginning improvisors will find that the approach in this book allows them to quickly begin applying the Aeolian mode to simple chord progressions.

This book explores the Aeolian mode and its use in jazz improvisation. It assumes that you are comfortable with the basic melodic and harmonic material presented in *Jazz Piano Vocabulary Volume 1: The Major Scale*. If not, you may wish to begin there. If this book is too elementary for you, you may want to take a look at *Volume 2: The Dorian Mode* or more advanced volumes such as *Volume 3: The Phrygian Mode*.

Like the other books in this series, this book offers a workbook approach to jazz improvisation with melodic examples that you can practice. You can listen to these examples on the Muse Eek website as well. The goal is to provide you with enough guidance to work confidently on your own so that you become comfortable integrating the scales into your improvisation.

This book is part of a series (available as e-books or in paper format) that will focus on learning and applying jazz scales in order to give you the vocabulary and skill to become a fluid jazz improvisor.

Muse Eek Publishing has created a website with a FAQ forum for this book. If you get stuck, or have questions or feedback, please contact me at Roberta@muse-eek.com and I will be happy to respond in the forum.

Roberta Piket
Brooklyn, New York

How To Use This Book

The material in this section has already been presented in previous volumes of the *Jazz Piano Vocabulary* series. If you have studied any of those books you may wish to skip this section. You may find it useful to review, however, in order to brush up on your practice habits.

This series of books assumes that you know how to read music and that you have a basic understanding of the diatonic (major/minor) system. As I mentioned in the foreword, if you are still struggling with these issues you may wish to begin with a different volume. If you need to brush up on your note-reading or diatonic scales, there is an extensive primer in *Jazz Piano Vocabulary: Volume 1 - The Major Scale* on note-reading, intervals, triads, seventh chords and rhythmic notation. If you find anything in this book confusing, please visit the Muse Eek web site at www.muse-eek.com first and check the FAQ section for this book to see if your question has already been answered. If not, use the form on the website to e-mail your questions.

The purpose of this book is to help you learn to improvise using the Aeolian mode. Memorize the scales and fingerings and practice the exercises repeatedly until you have mastered them. Execute each example at the piano slowly and carefully to begin. Increase your tempo gradually as your ability increases. Make sure you use the exact same fingerings every time so that you can learn the scales efficiently as your hand builds muscle memory.

You may wish to use a metronome to be certain that you are not slowing down on difficult passages. Try putting the metronome on the "two and four"; that is, the second and fourth beats of each measure. This emphasis on the "weak" beats instead of the "strong" first and third beats is part of what gives jazz its unique rhythmic character. If it is too difficult for you to play with the metronome on two and four, then first learn the scales with the metronome on the quarter note and then, after you are comfortable with the notes, try the "two and four" again. Eventually it will get easier to feel the music this way and your sense of rhythm will become stronger and more sophisticated.

Play through each exercise smoothly and evenly. As you master each exercise you should gradually increase the tempo while still maintaining complete control. This will help you to develop good habits which will remain with you when you start playing more technically challenging music.

This book contains a great deal of material. You will not be able to learn everything in the book in one sitting. Depending on how fluent you are with scales in general, it may take you anywhere from a few weeks to several months or more to truly master the material in this book. Spend as much time as you need on each concept until you have truly mastered it.

Consistency is critical. Even if you have less time on some days than on other days, it is extremely important that you refresh your memory almost every day until the material is completely absorbed. If you do this, you will find that you will progress much more steadily and will save yourself a great deal of frustration.

In the same vein, it is also a good idea to go back to previous material even while moving forward through the book. This will help reinforce what you've already learned, enabling you to build on it. For example, if you have learned the first six Aeolian scales and are working on the seventh, you may want to play through the first six at least once a day until they become second nature so that you don't forget them.

Swung Eighth Notes

Each scale is presented in an eighth note pattern (resolving to a quarter note at the top and bottom) to allow for an even four-bar phrase as the scale ascends and descends. If you are comfortable doing so, try to play each exercise with *swung eighth notes* so that this type of feel can become second nature to you. In swung (or "swinging") eighth notes, the first eighth note in a pair of eighth notes is held twice as long as the second eighth note, giving the notes a relaxed triplet feel. Eighth notes are almost always interpreted in jazz music as *swung*. For example, note the following phrase:

Example 4

In a jazz context, this would be played as:

Obviously, it would be very cumbersome to write every single eighth note pair in a lead sheet as a triplet. For this reason, in jazz it is assumed that the eighth-note is swung unless otherwise noted. Two exceptions to this rule are Brazilian jazz and Latin jazz where it is understood that the eighth notes are *straight* (that is, not swung).

A sound file illustrating this example has been provided on the Muse Eek website under this book's title.

Order of Presentation

The scales are ordered by key using the *circle of fifths*. The circle of fifths allows us to progress through all the keys by moving either up or down in perfect fifths from one key to the next.

In the scales section of this book we will progress up in fifths, from A Aeolian to E Aeolian to B Aeolian, etc., until we arrive at D Aeolian.

Fingering

It is important to use the correct fingering when learning the scales. If you are inconsistent in your fingering you will find it difficult to build muscle memory which will make it more difficult to internalize the material.

Recall that the thumb of each hand is always "1", and the pinky is always "5". If you can remember this then you will quickly become proficient at applying the correct fingerings as you learn to play a passage of written music.

Particularly if you are self-taught, some of these fingerings may at first seem awkward. Give yourself a chance to get used to them. After learning them, if something still feels awkward, you can change it. Everyone's hand is different. However, don't assume they don't work if they feel "funny" the first time you try them. Practice them slowly, making sure to apply them accurately and consistently. Only by applying the correct fingerings every time you play will using them become automatic. Eventually, with enough experience, you will be able to determine the correct fingering on your own.

Introduction To The Aeolian Mode

The modes that developed in Europe during the Medieval period are surprisingly useful in jazz improvisation. These modes are sometimes known as the "Church modes" because they evolved through the use of Gregorian chant, the sacred monophonic music of Europe's Catholic Church during this period. The Church modes are derived from the Major scale. That is, each mode has the same notes as the Major scale, but each mode starts and ends on a different note from the Major scale. The seven modes that we use in jazz are: Ionian, Dorian, Phrygian, Lydian, Mixolydian, Aeolian, and Locrian.

This book is concerned with the Aeolian mode. You may already know that the *Dorian* mode can be used to solo on a minor 7th chord. In this book we will see how it is possible to solo over an *entire* minor key progression using just one Aeolian mode.

The terms "Aeolian mode" and "natural minor scale" refer to the exact same scale. (You may not be familiar with the three types of minor scales: natural minor, harmonic minor, and melodic minor. While they are a necessary component of any modern jazz musician's vocabulary, the harmonic and melodic minor scales are beyond the scope of this book.) In this book we will sometimes use the term "Aeolian mode" amd sometimes use the term "natural minor", depending on the context.

The Aeolian mode can be derived by starting and ending on the sixth note of the major scale. For example, if we wanted to figure out the notes for A Aeolian, we would remember that A is the sixth note of the C major scale. Therefore, the A Aeolian mode starts on A and contains all the notes in the C major scale from A to A:

A Aeolian Mode

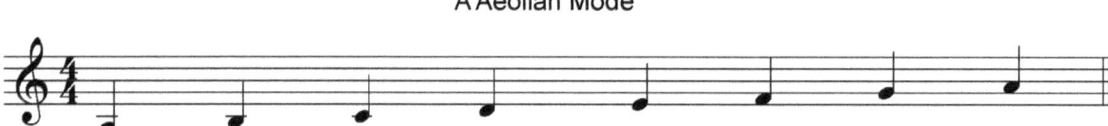

Because A natural minor contains the same notes as C major, we say that the key of A minor is the *relative minor* of C major. We can also say that C major is the *relative major* of A minor. So another way to figure out the notes of a particular natural minor scale is to think of the relative major of that scale.

Remember that the relative major is a *minor third above* its relative minor and the relative minor is a *minor third below* it's relative major. For example, E natural minor is the relative minor of G major. (I.e., it contains the same notes as G major.) It is a minor third below G major.

E Aeolian Mode

Another way to think of the Aeolian mode is in terms of its sequence of whole steps and half steps. (A half step is the distance between two notes that are right next to each other on the piano, such as A and B♭, or B and C. A whole step is simply two half steps. Major and minor scales, and the modes derived from these scales, always consist of combinations of these two intervals. (For a more detailed explanation of these fundamental music theory concepts please examine the theory primer at the beginning of *Volume 1* of this series.)) The pattern of steps for any Aeolian mode in any key is the same:

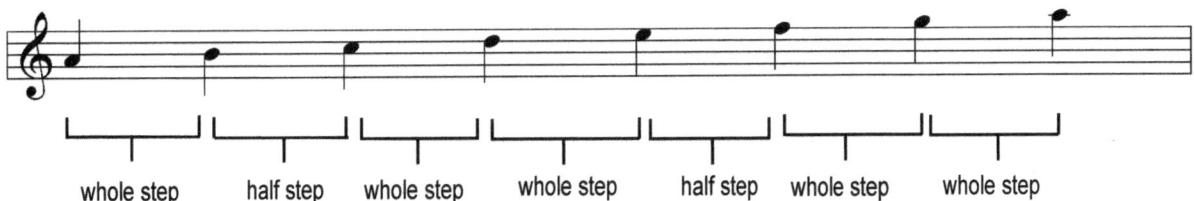

Applying The Aeolian Mode To Improvisation

In other books in this series we have discussed how to apply a given mode to a specific chord. However, in deciding what mode to use, it is important to look at the context in which the chord appears. In this book we will think about the Aeolian mode not just as a way to improvise over a minor 7th chord, but as a way to think about approaching an entire chord progression. If you are a beginning improvisor you will find that the natural minor scale will get you started playing the right notes over minor key progressions.

Try to play through the examples in this section *in time* so that you can hear how the differences in harmonic rhythm (how quickly the chords change) affects the tonality. Audio files of these examples can also be found on the Muse-Eek website.

Let's start our improvising journey with the simplest progression of all - a single chord. We will use the key of C minor for now, but everything we discuss here of course applies to all minor keys. (In case you have forgotten, the symbol ∕. indicates that you are to play the same chord as in the previous measure.)

If you play this "progression", you can easily hear that we are improvising in the key of C minor. You may recall from Volume One of this series that we say that the chord built on the first note of the key is called the *tonic* chord. Therefore, in this case, the C minor 7 chord is the "tonic" chord or the i chord ("one chord") in the key of C minor. (If you do not understand the use of these Roman numerals please see *Volume One* of *Jazz Piano Vocabulary*.) When we are in a minor key, we can use the Aeolian mode (also called the natural minor scale) to improvise over the tonic chord. Here is an example of how it might sound to use the Aeolian mode to solo over its corresponding minor chord:

Example 2

Now let's look at a chord progression in a minor key that uses the i chord and the iv chord. In the key of C minor, of course, the i chord would be C minor 7 and the iv chord would be F minor 7.

Here we have a choice regarding what mode to use. In a chord progression like this, you will most likely hear each minor 7th chord relating to it's corresponding Dorian scale; that is, C Dorian for the C minor 7 chord and F Dorian for the F minor 7 chord. Using these scales, you might play something like this:

Example 3

If you are not fluid switching from mode to mode yet, a simpler option is to use C aeolian mode for the entire progression:

Example 4

Practice soloing over the i-iv progression illustrated in examples 3 and 4 using the aeolian scale. Then transpose the progression and try to play over it in all keys. To help you along, the progression has been transposed into the remaining 11 keys below.

Key of G minor (Use G Aeolian)

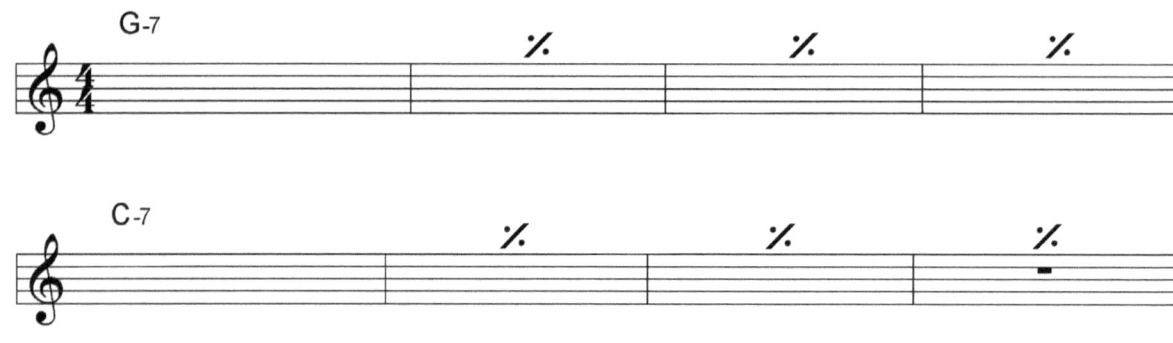

Key of D minor (Use D Aeolian)

Key of A minor (Use A Aeolian)

Key of E minor (Use E Aeolian)

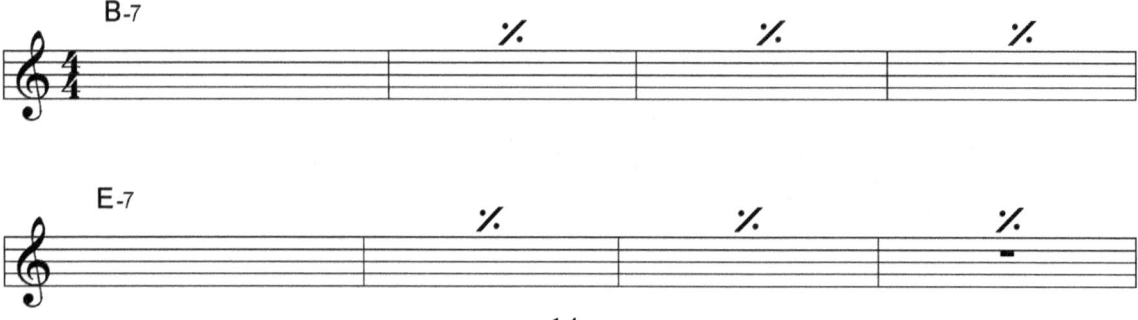

Key of B minor (Use B Aeolian)

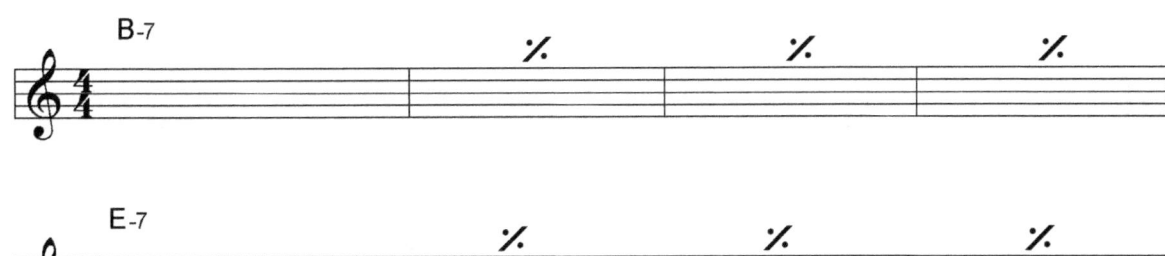

Key of F# minor (Use F# Aeolian)

Key of C# minor (Use C# Aeolian)

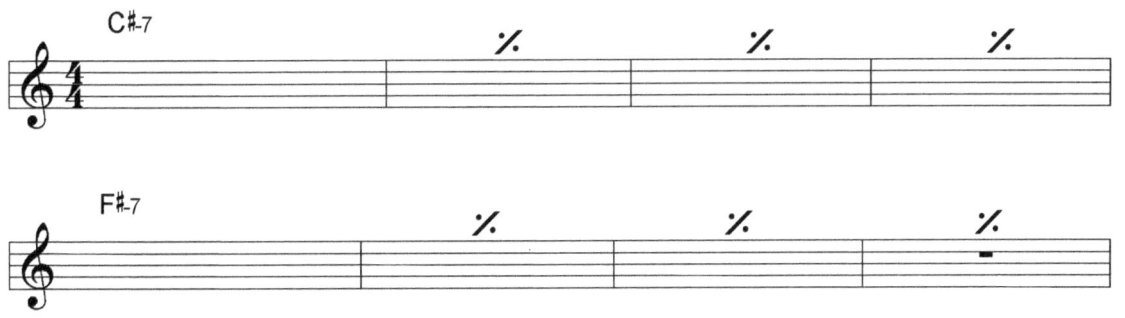

Key of Ab minor (Use Ab Aeolian)

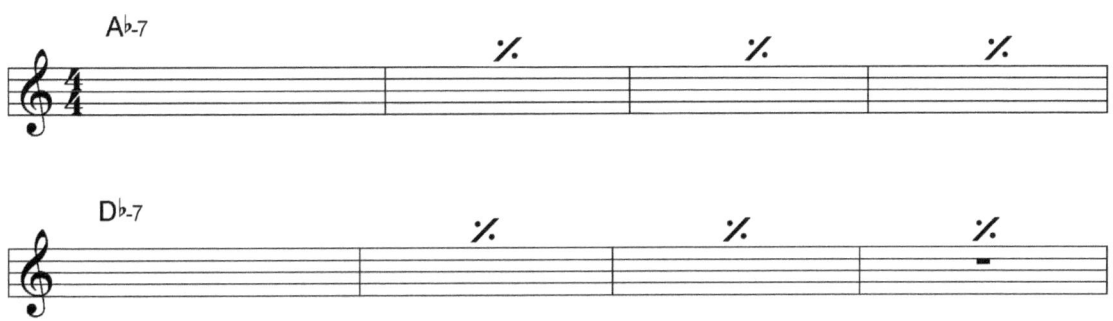

Key of E♭ minor (Use E♭ Aeolian)

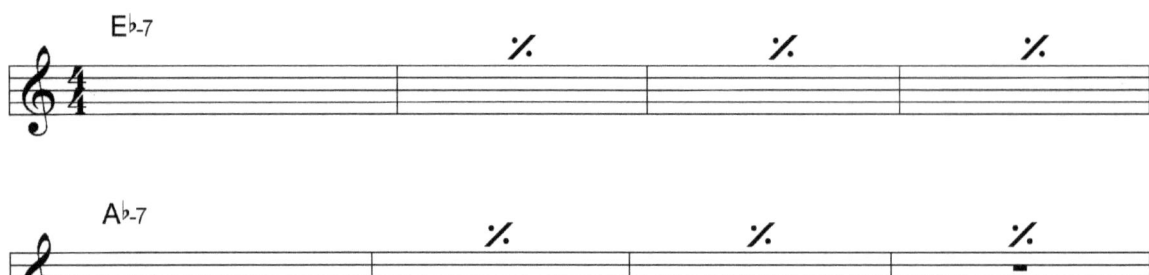

Key of B♭ minor (Use B♭ Aeolian)

Key of F minor (Use F Aeolian)

In the i-iv chord progression we just worked on, we had a choice of using the Dorian or Aeolian mode. Look at the following minor chord vamp centered around C minor 7. Unlike the previous example, the iv chord in this example is used only as a passing chord. (A passing chord is a chord which we can insert before a functional chord in order to create more harmonic movement and interest:)

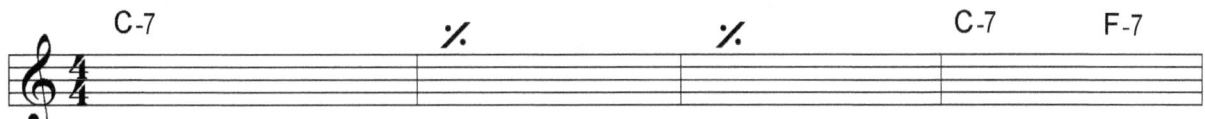

In a case like this, it is not practical to think of a different scale for the two beats of F minor 7 because the F minor 7 chord goes by so quickly. It makes more sense to use one chord over the entire progression. We cannot use C Dorian over the entire progression because the C Dorian scale will not fit over the F minor 7 chord. If you look at the C Dorian scale below you will see the the sixth note of the C Dorian scale is A, which would result in a major third on the F minor 7 chord:

C Dorian Scale

However, flatting the sixth note of the C Dorian scale gives us the C Aeolian scale: Now the scale will fit over both the C minor 7 and the F minor 7 chords.

C Aeolian Scale

Look at the scale below. As you can see, C Aeolian contains the same notes as F Dorian.

Instead of having to switch modes for one measure, thinking in Aeolian is a simple way to tackle minor progressions with i- and iv- chords. Here is an example of soloing over this progression using only C Aeolian mode:

Example 4

Left Hand Chords: "Shell" Voicings

In the other books in this series, I've included some rootless left-hand jazz voicings to learn while practicing the mode. I haven't done that in this book for two reasons. First, it's been my experience that beginning improvisors are best off practing soloing with the right hand without adding in the left hand right away. The second reason releates to the fact that the Aeolian mode corresponds to the natural minor scale, I believe that it is important to learn the minor scales in both hands, just as you have (hopefully) done with your major scales.

When you are ready to add in the left hand, you will want to start with simple left hand voicings, perhaps simple "shell" voicings, which are essentially 7th chord voicings that leave out the fifth of the chord.

Why do we leave the fifth out of the voicing in shell voicings? The reason is that the fifth is not an identifying note in the chord. While the third and seventh give us identifying information about the *chord quality* (e.g., major 7th, minor 7th, dominant 7th), the fifth gives us no information as it is the same in all three of these chord qualities.

Here is an example of a shell voicing. Notice the voicing contains a root, third and seventh but no fifth.

Here is a simple ii-V-I progression using two-note shell voicings. Each voicings consists of the root and either the 3rd or the 7th. (Notice how the non-root note always moves to the closest note possible in the next chord. This concept of chord tones moving smoothly with as few jumps as possible from note to note is called *voice leading*.)

Here is a simple major ii-V-I progression using two-note shell voicings. Each voicings consists of the root and either the 3rd or the 7th. Observe how the non-root note always moves to the closest note possible in the next chord. This concept of chord tones moving smoothly with as few jumps as possible from note to note is called *voice leading*. In a typical ii-V-I progression, the 7th of the ii chord becomes the 3rd of the V chord which becomes the 7th of the I chord:

Major ii-V-I Shell Voicings

Major ii-V-I progressions are not directly related to the Aeolian mode. However, if you don't already know your major ii-V-I shell voicings, you might want to learn them before tackling the minor ii-V-i's. To facilitate this, all twelve major ii-V-I shell voicings are illustrated below.

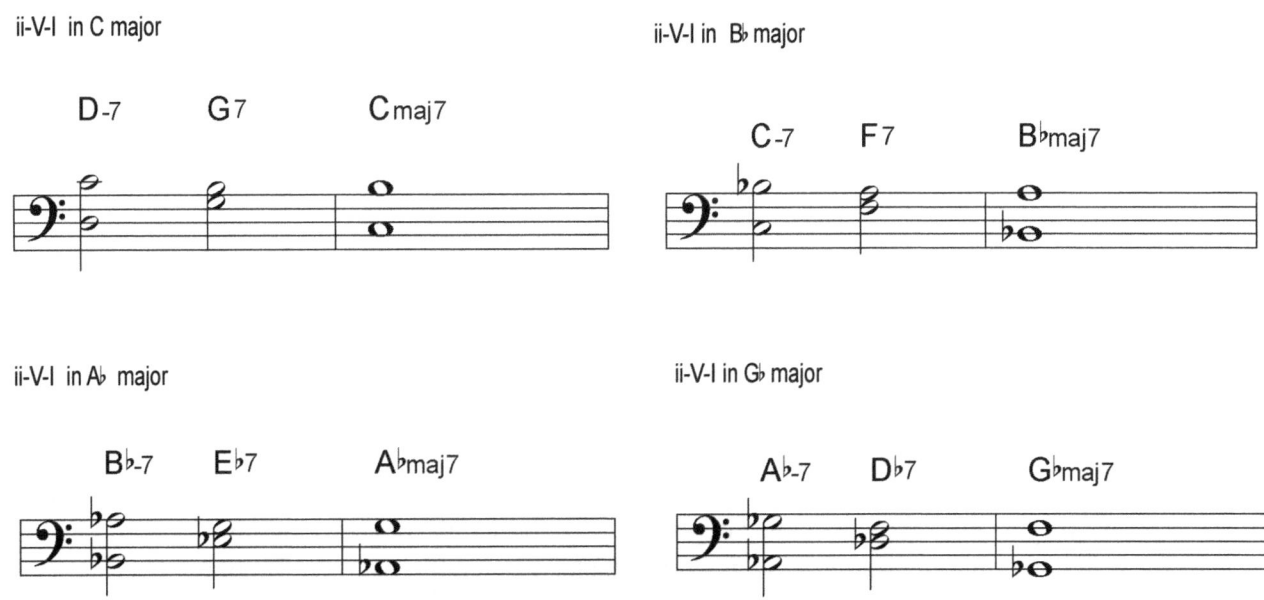

ii-V-I in E major

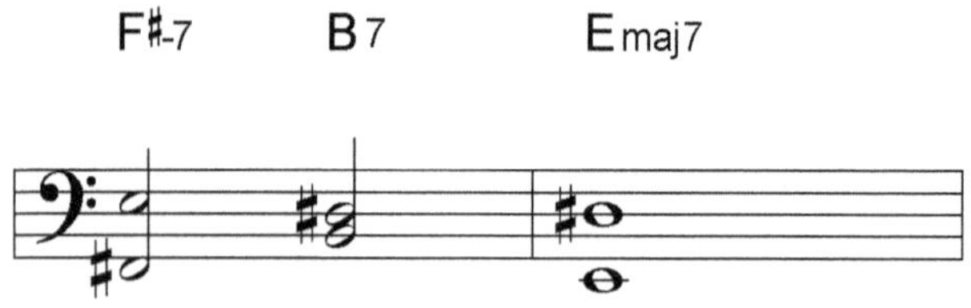

ii-V-I in D major

ii-V-I in B major

ii-V-I in A major

ii-V-I in G major

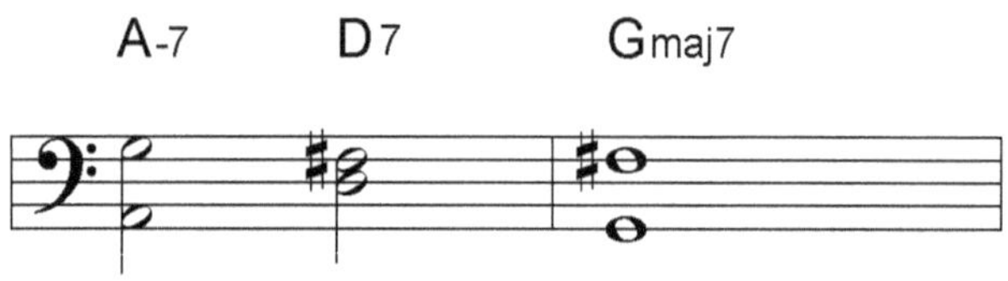

ii-V-I in F major

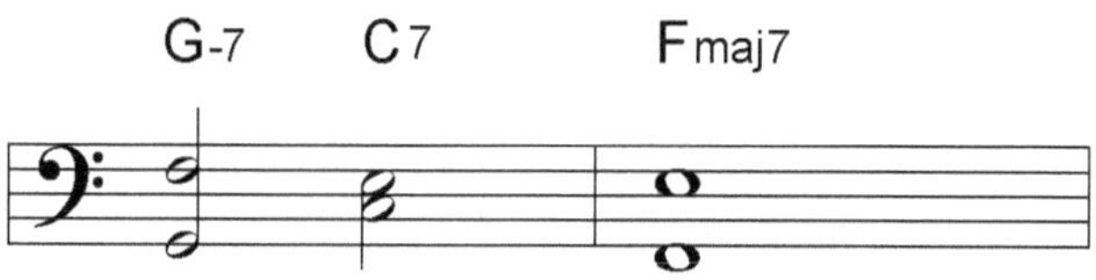

ii-V-I in E♭ major

ii-V-I in D♭ major

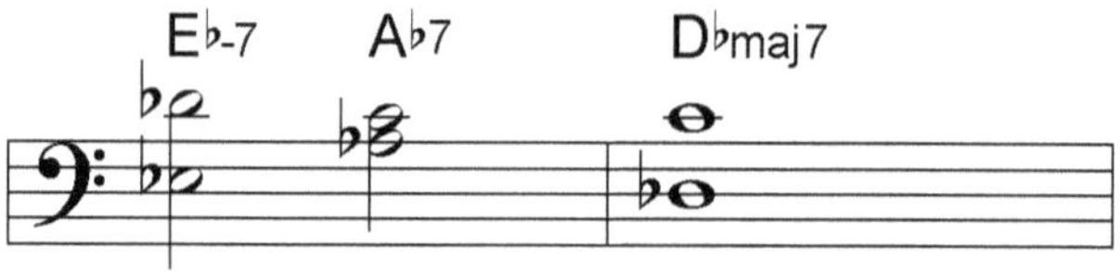

Now let's play a minor ii-V-i progression using shell voicings.

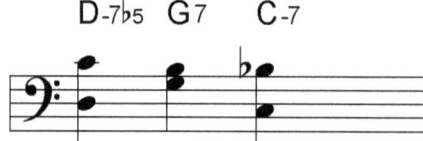

Note that the ii chord in a minor key has a flatted fifth. Since this is a distinguishing characteristic of this chord, we might choose to make an exception to our "no fifth" rule, and include the fifth in the ii-7♭5 chord. Whether to play the fifth is a matter of taste. You should become fluent playing the progression either way.

Minor ii-V-i Shell Voicings

Memorize the following minor ii-V-i shell voicings so that you can play them automatically in your left hand:

ii-V-i in C minor

ii-V-i in B♭ minor

ii-V-i in A♭ minor

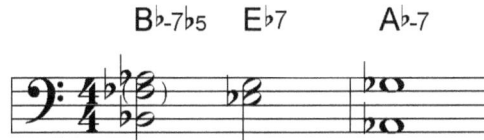

ii-V-i in G♭ minor

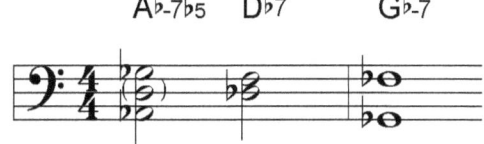

ii-V-i in E minor

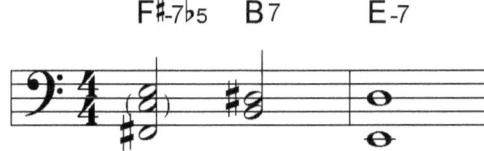

ii-V-i in D minor

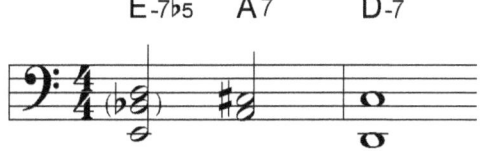

ii-V-i in B minor

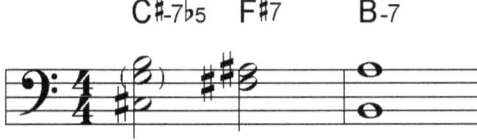

ii-V-i in A minor

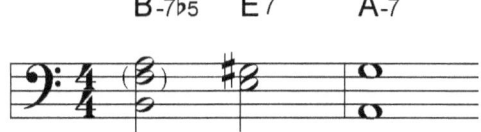

ii-V-i in G minor

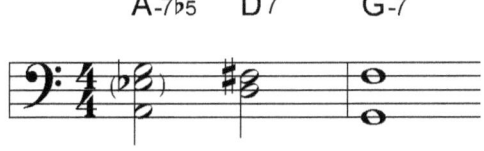

ii-V-i in F minor

ii-V-i in E♭ minor   ii-V-i in D♭ minor

When playing the minor ii-V-i progression., you can apply the Aeolian mode that corresponds to the key of the progression. For example, in playing a ii-V-i progression in C minor, you would use the C Aeolian mode.

The following example ilustrates how to practice the Aeolian mode over the corresponding minor ii-V-i progression. You can hear this example on the Muse-Eek website:

Example 6

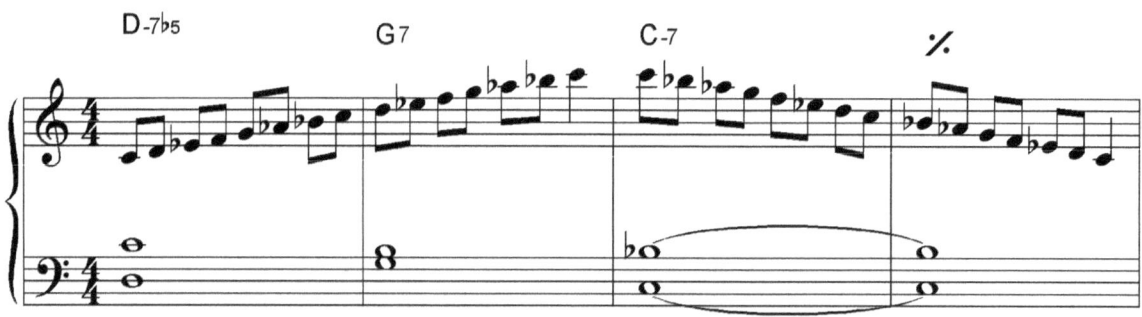

After you are comfortable playing each Aeolian mode in the next section of this book, practice them in your right hand, while playing the minor ii-V-i progression in your left hand as illustrated in Example 6. A sound sample of this example and others in this book can be found on the Muse Eek website.

Later we'll illustrate how the notes of the Aeolian mode correspond to the chord tones in this progression.

Aeolian Modes with Fingerings

Before you start learning the Aeolian mode in all keys, here are a few suggestions and guidelines to help you get the most out of your practice time. If you have already reviewed these suggestions in other volumes of this series you can skip this section and go right to the scales.

Hand Position

It is important to develop good habits with respect to hand position. It may not seem important when playing slowly, but when you begin to execute faster passages, you will find that good hand and wrist position will make a diference in your control, thus affecting your ability to play evenly and cleanly.

When playing notes that are close together, as is the case with scales, fingers should be bent, so that you are playing with the balls of your fingers. (If you have long finger nails you will need to cut them to achieve this.) All fingers should be kept in this rounded position whether you are using them or not. (See the picture below.) Of course if you are playing a widely spread chord, you fingers will not be as bent as they are when playing a scale where all the notes are under one hand position and you don't have to stretch your fingers. The idea is to keep your fingers in a gently bent yet relaxed position.

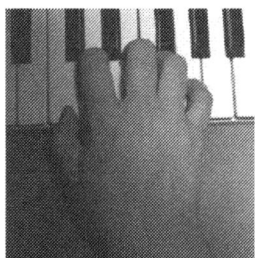

Many inexperienced pianists veer their wrists from side to side, particularly when changing hand position during a scale. (For example, switching from the fourth finger back to one as your right hand ascends.) This is called ulnar deviation and is a great way to develop wrist tendonitis (a bad thing). When switching to your thumb, do NOT change your wrist position relative to your hand. Instead, as you glide up (or down) the keyboard, bring your thumb under you hand and reach for the note. Let your thumb do the work, not your wrist.

To begin, practice each scale in the right and left hands separately, up two octaves and down two octaves, paying attention to the fingering provided. You may find it useful to say each note out loud as you play. Even better for your ear is to try and sing the notes of each scale while playing.

Swung Eight Notes, Articulation and Phrasing

Playing these scales with a swung eighth note feel (as explained in the "How To Use This Book" section), will help you to develop a more authentically "jazz" rhythmic feel. As you become more comfortable with the actual notes of each scale and chord, you should begin to focus more on the subtleties of articulation.

Each scale should be played legato, meaning that the notes are connected. Many jazz piano students make the mistake of trying to play too staccato, because of the percussive nature of jazz. On the other hand, do *not* use the damper or sustain pedal when playing medium tempo or faster jazz eighth note lines. This is another common error made by inexperienced pianists. An audio file of what these scales should sound like is provided on this book's page at the Muse-Eek web site.

The Modes

A Aeolian

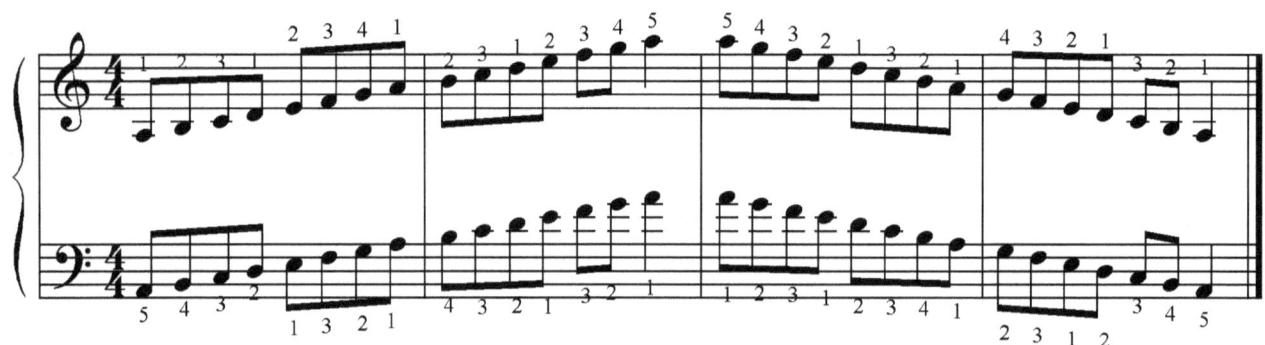

E Aeolian

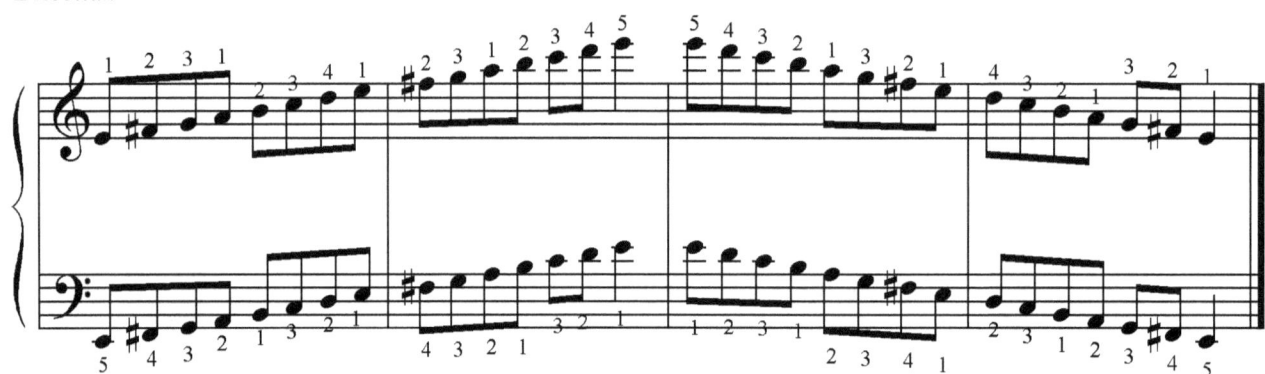

B Aeolian

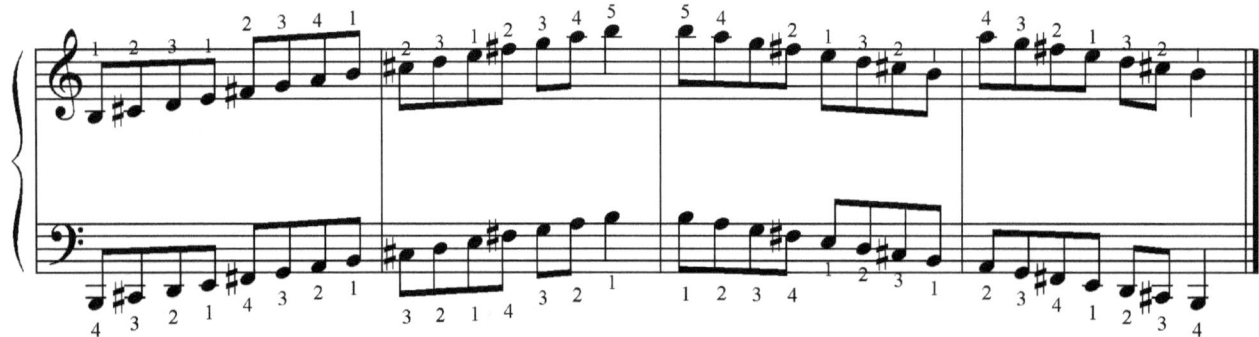

F# Aeolian

C# Aeolian

G# Aeolian

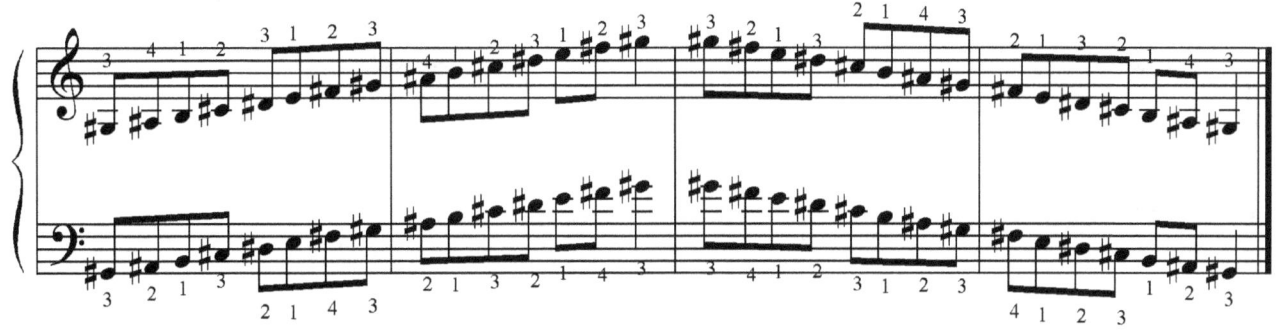

E♭ Aeolian

Bb Aeolian

F Aeolian

C Aeolian

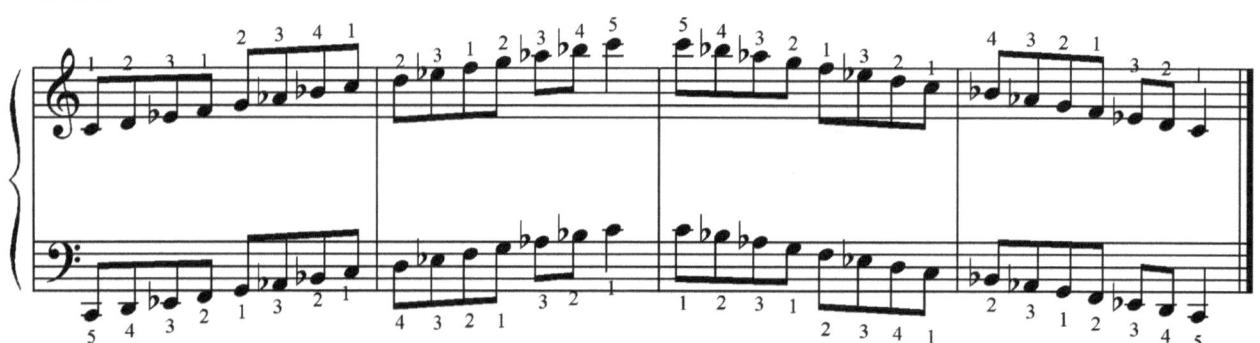

G Aeolian

D Aeolian

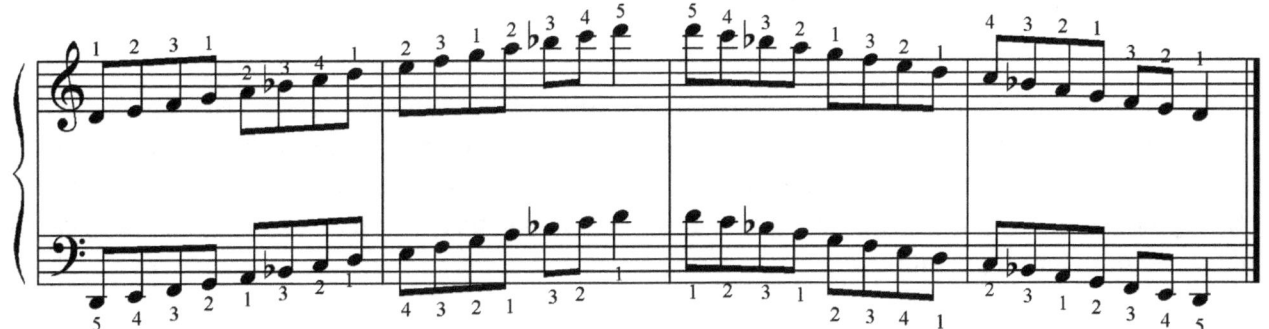

The Minor Blues Progression

Here's a simple way to start soloing over a minor blues. Just play the Aeolian mode that corresponds to the key you're in. To illustrate this, below is a 12-bar blues in C minor. We will get to an example of a solo over this form in a moment. For now, play the C Aeolian mode over the entire form with your right hand while playing the chords in your left hand, as illustrated below. This is so that you can clearly hear the scale against all the chords of the progression.

We've already discussed in this book why the tonic chord's Aeolian mode (C minor in this case) works over the iv chord (F minor). Let's look at the ii chord in bar 9. In this measure we have a D-7b5. The example below illustrates how each note in the C Aeolian scale relates to a D-7b5 chord. You can see from this example that all the notes in C Aeolian will work over the D-7b5. (If you are already familiar with the Locrian scale, you may find it interesting that C Aeolian contains the same notes as the D Locrian mode. If you are not yet familiar with the Locrian mode, don't worry about it yet.)

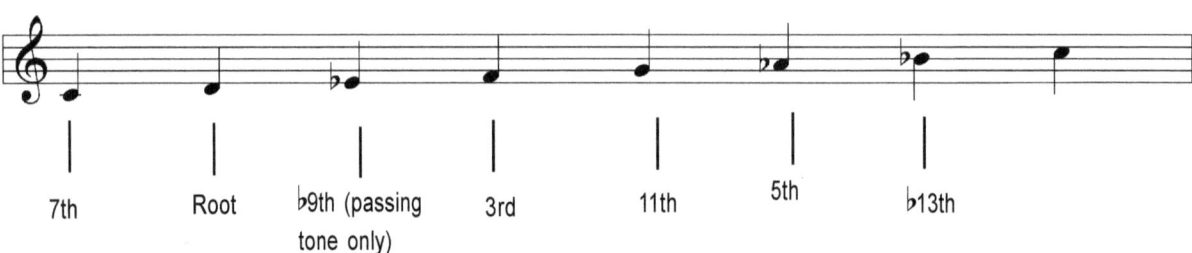

There is an exception to using the Aeolian mode on a minor blues. In a minor key, sometimes a bVI7 chord is substituted for the ii chord. So the last four bars of the minor blues chord progression would look like this (notice the Ab7 instead of D-7b5):

In this case, the C Aeolian mode won't work, because in the C Aeolian mode there is a G, which would give us a major seventh (G) against the dominant 7th (Gb) of the Ab7 chord.

If you see a bVI7 chord on the ninth bar of a minor blues when soloing, you have two choices. You can play a different scale over that chord, such as Ab Mixolydian, since a Mixolydian scale will always work over a dominant seventh chord; or, if you are the only chordal instrument playing, you can play a ii-7b5 chord instead of the bVI7 chord.

The final chord to address in the minor blues is the V7 chord in bar 10. Below is an analysis of the chord tones and tensions we get by playing C Aeolian against the G7 chord.

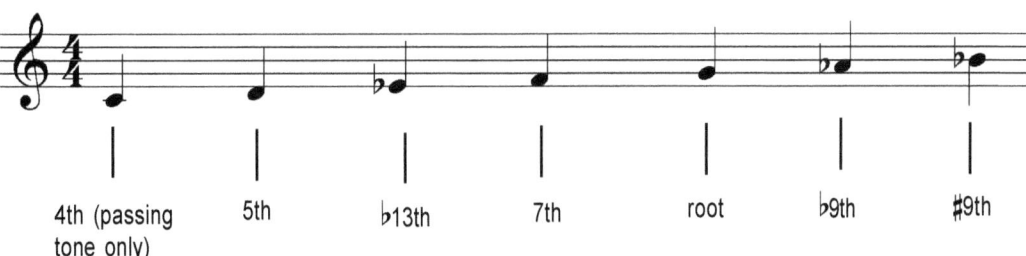

You may notice that in this scale there is no 3rd in realtion to the G7 chord. The #9 and b9 without the major third give the scale a bluesy sound again this chord.

Here is an example of a solo using C Aeolian over a C minor blues. You can hear this example at the Muse-Eek web site. Listen to how the same scale sounds different when applied to the different chords.

Example 5

Practice using the Aeolian scale with minor blues in all keys. For example, practice playing over an F minor blues using the F aeolian mode, then practice playing over a G minor blues using the G Aeolian mode, etc., until you are comfortable using all the modes and playing the minor blues form in every key.

Further Exploration

If you have mastered the Aeolian mode, you are ready to move on to the other modes, such as the Dorian and Mixolydian.

This book is part of a series that focuses on learning and applying jazz scales in order to give you the vocabulary and confidence to become a fluid jazz improvisor. When you are ready to delve further into the modes to develop your improvisational ability, you may wish to build on the progress you've made with another book in this series, such as *Volume 2: The Dorian Mode*, or *Volume 5: The Mixolydian Mode*. These books go into greater theoretical detail as your confidence and ability to absorb more material grows. They include etudes, rhythmic and phrasing exercises and left-hand rootless voicings.

If you have any questions or concerns that have not been addressed in this book, feel free to contact me through the FAQ for this book at the Muse-Eek website, www.muse-eek.com.

Books Available From
Muse Eek Publishing Company

The Bruce Arnold series of instruction books for guitar are the result of 30 years of teaching. Mr. Arnold, who teaches at New York University and Princeton University has listened to the questions and problems of his students, and written over fifty books addressing the needs of the beginning to advanced student. Written in a direct, friendly and practical manner, each book is structured in such a way as to enable a student to understand, retain and apply musical information. In short, these books teach.

1st Steps for a Beginning Guitarist
Spiral Bound ISBN 1890944-90-4   Perfect Bound ISBN 1890944-93-9

1st Steps for a Beginning Guitarist is a comprehensive method for guitar students who have no prior musical training. Whether you are playing acoustic, electric or twelve-string guitar, this book will give you the information you need, and trouble shoot the various pitfalls that can hinder the self-taught musician. Includes pictures, videos and audio in the form of midifiles and mp3's.

Chord Workbook for Guitar Volume 1 (2nd edition)
Spiral Bound ISBN 0-9648632-1-9   Perfect Bound ISBN 1890944-50-5

A consistent seller, this book addresses the needs of the beginning through intermediate student. The beginning student will learn chords on the guitar, and a section is also included to help learn the basics of music theory. Progressions are provided to help the student apply these chords to common sequences. The more advanced student will find the reharmonization section to be an invaluable resource of harmonic choices. Information is given through musical notation as well as tablature.

Chord Workbook for Guitar Volume 2 (2nd edition)
Spiral Bound ISBN 0-9648632-3-5   Perfect Bound ISBN 1890944-51-3

This book is the Rosetta Stone of pop/jazz chords, and is geared to the intermediate to advanced student. These are the chords that any serious student bent on a musical career must know. Unlike other books which simply give examples of isolated chords, this unique book provides a comprehensive series of progressions and chord combinations which are immediately applicable to both composition and performance.

Music Theory Workbook for Guitar Series

The worlds most popular instrument, the guitar, is not taught in our public schools. In addition, it is one of the hardest on which to learn the basics of music. As a result, it is frequently difficult for the serious guitarist to get a firm foundation in theory.

Theory Workbook for Guitar Volume 1
Spiral Bound ISBN 0-9648632-4-3   Perfect Bound ISBN 1890944-52-1

This book provides real hands-on application of intervals and chords. A theory section written in concise and easy to understand language prepares the student for all exercises. Worksheets are given that quiz a student about intervals and chord construction using staff notation and guitar tablature. Answers are supplied in the back of the book enabling a student to work without a teacher.

Theory Workbook for Guitar Volume 2
Spiral Bound ISBN 0-9648632-5-1   Perfect Bound ISBN 1890944-53-X

This book provides real hands-on application for 22 different scale types. A theory section written in concise and easy to understand language prepares the student for all exercises. Worksheets are given that quiz a student about scale construction using staff notation and guitar tablature. Answers are supplied in the back of the book enabling a student to work without a teacher. Audio files are also available on the muse-eek.com website to facilitate practice and improvisation with all the scales presented.

Rhythm Book Series

These books are a breakthrough in music instruction, using the internet as a teaching tool! Audio files of all the exercises are easily downloaded from the internet.

Rhythm Primer
Spiral Bound ISBN 0-890944-03-3   Perfect Bound ISBN 1890944-59-9

This 61 page book concentrates on all basic rhythms using four rhythmic levels. All examples use one pitch, allowing the student to focus completely on time and rhythm. All exercises can be downloaded from the internet to facilitate learning. See http://www.muse-eek.com for details

Rhythms Volume 1
Spiral Bound ISBN 0-9648632-7-8   Perfect Bound ISBN 1890944-55-6

This 120 page book concentrates on eighth note rhythms and is a thesaurus of rhythmic patterns. All examples use one pitch, allowing the student to focus completely on time and rhythm. All exercises can be downloaded from the internet to facilitate learning. See http://www.muse-eek.com for details.

Rhythms Volume 2
Spiral Bound ISBN 0-9648632-8-6   Perfect Bound ISBN 1890944-56-4

This volume concentrates on sixteenth note rhythms, and is a 108 page thesaurus of rhythmic patterns. All examples use one pitch, allowing the student to focus completely on time and rhythm. All exercises can be downloaded from the internet to facilitate learning. See http://www.muse-eek.com for details.

Rhythms Volume 3
Spiral Bound ISBN 0-890944-04-1   Perfect Bound ISBN 1890944-57-2

This volume concentrates on thirty second note rhythms, and is a 102 page thesaurus of rhythmic patterns. All examples use one pitch, allowing the student to focus completely on time and rhythm. All exercises can be downloaded from the internet to facilitate learning. See http://www.muse-eek.com for details.

Odd Meters Volume 1
Spiral Bound ISBN 0-9648632-9-4   Perfect Bound ISBN 1890944-58-0

This book applies both eighth and sixteenth note rhythms to odd meter combinations. All examples use one pitch, allowing the student to focus completely on time and rhythm. Exercises can be downloaded from the internet to facilitate learning. This 100 page book is an essential sight reading tool. See http://www.muse-eek.com for details.

Contemporary Rhythms Volume 1
Spiral Bound ISBN 1-890944-27-0   Perfect Bound ISBN 1890944-84-X

This volume concentrates on eight note rhythms and is a thesaurus of rhythmic patterns. Each exercise uses one pitch which allows the student to focus completely on time and rhythm. Exercises use modern innovations common to twentieth century notation, thereby familiarizing the student with the most sophisticated systems likely to be encountered in the course of a musical career. All exercises can be downloaded from the internet to facilitate learning. See http://www.muse-eek.com for details.

Contemporary Rhythms Volume 2
Spiral Bound ISBN 1-890944-28-9   Perfect Bound ISBN 1890944-85-8

This volume concentrates on sixteenth note rhythms and is a thesaurus of rhythmic patterns. Each exercise uses one pitch which allows the student to focus completely on time and rhythm. Exercise use modern innovations common to twentieth century notation, thereby familiarizing the student with the most sophisticated systems likely to be encountered in the course of a musical career. All exercises can be downloaded from the internet to facilitate learning. See http://www.muse-eek.com for details.

Independence Volume 1
Spiral Bound ISBN 1-890944-00-9   Perfect Bound ISBN 1890944-83-1

This 51 page book is designed for pianists, stick and touchstyle guitarists, percussionists and anyone who wishes to develop the rhythmic independence of their hands. This volume concentrates on quarter, eighth and sixteenth note rhythms and is a thesaurus of rhythmic patterns. The exercises in this book gradually incorporate more and more complex rhythmic patterns making it an excellent tool for both the beginning and the advanced student.

Other Guitar Study Aids

Right Hand Technique for Guitar Volume 1
Spiral Bound ISBN 0-9648632-6-X   Perfect Bound ISBN 1890944-54-8

Heres a breakthrough in music instruction, using the internet as a teaching tool! This book gives a concise method for developing right hand technique on the guitar, one of the most overlooked and under-addressed aspects of learning the instrument. The simplest, most basic movements are used to build fatigue-free technique. Exercises can be downloaded from the internet to facilitate learning. See http://www.muse-eek.com for details.

Single String Studies Volume One
Spiral Bound ISBN 1-890944-01-7   Perfect Bound ISBN 1890944-62-9

This book is an excellent learning tool for both the beginner who has no experience reading music on the guitar, and the advanced student looking to improve their ledger line reading and general knowledge of each string of the guitar. Each exercise concentrates the students attention on one string at a time. This allows a familiarity to form between the written pitch and where it can be found on the guitar along with improving ones feel for jumping linearly across the fretboard. Exercises can be downloaded from the internet to facilitate learning. See http://www.muse-eek.com for details.

Single String Studies Volume Two
Spiral Bound ISBN 1-890944-05-X   Perfect Bound ISBN 1890944-64-5

    This book is a continuation of Volume One, but using non-diatonic notes. Volume Two helps the intermediate and advanced student improve their ledger line reading and general knowledge of each string of the guitar. Each exercise concentrates the students attention on one string at a time. This allows a familiarity to form between the written pitch and where it can be found on the guitar along with improving ones feel for jumping linearly across the fretboard. Exercises can be downloaded from the internet to facilitate learning. See http://www.muse-eek.com for details.

Single String Studies Volume One (Bass Clef)
Spiral Bound ISBN 1-890944-02-5   Perfect Bound ISBN 1890944-63-7

    This book is an excellent learning tool for both the beginner who has no experience reading music on the bass guitar, and the advanced student looking to improve their ledger line reading and general knowledge of each string of the bass. Each exercise concentrates a students attention of one string at a time. This allows a familiarity to form between the written pitch and where it can be found on the bass along with improving ones feel for jumping linearly across the fretboard. Exercises can be downloaded from the internet to facilitate learning. See http://www.muse-eek.com for details.

Single String Studies Volume Two (Bass Clef)
Spiral Bound ISBN 1-890944-06-8   Perfect Bound ISBN 1890944-65-3

    This book is a continuation of Volume One, but using non-diatonic notes. Volume Two helps the intermediate and advanced student improve their ledger line reading and general knowledge of each string of the bass. Each exercise concentrates the students attention on one string at a time. This allows a familiarity to form between the written pitch and where it can be found on the bass along with improving ones feel for jumping linearly across the fretboard. Exercises can be downloaded from the internet to facilitate learning. See http://www.muse-eek.com for details.

Guitar Clinic
Spiral Bound ISBN 1-890944-45-9   Perfect Bound ISBN 1890944-86-6

    Guitar Clinic contains techniques and exercises Mr. Arnold uses in the clinics and workshops he teaches around the U.S.. Much of the material in this book is culled from Mr. ArnoldÕs educational series, over thirty books in all. The student wishing to expand on his or her studies will find suggestions within the text as to which of Mr. Arnold's books will best serve their specific needs. Topics covered include: how to read music, sight reading, reading rhythms, music theory, chord and scale construction, modal sequencing, approach notes, reharmonization, bass and chord comping, and hexatonic scales.

The Essentials: Chord Charts, Scales, and Lead Patterns for the Guitar
Saddle Stitched (Stapled) ISBN 1-890944-94-7

    This book is truly essential to the aspiring guitarist. It includes the most commonly played chords on the guitar in all keys, plus a bonus of the most commonly used scales and lead patterns. You can quickly learn all the chords, scales and lead patterns you need to know to play your favorite songs-and solo over them, too! The Essentials doesn't stop there, though. It also includes chord progressions to help you learn how to chord songs in folk, country, rock, blues and other popular styles. The books contain loads of easy to understand diagrams of chords, scales and lead patterns so you will be up and running in no time!

Sight Singing and Ear Training Series

The world is full of ear training and sight reading books, so why do we need more? This sight singing and ear training series uses a different method of teaching relative pitch sight singing and ear training. The success of this method has been remarkable. Along with a new method of ear training these books also use CDs and the internet as a teaching tool! Audio files of all the exercises are easily downloaded from the internet at www.muse-eek.com By combining interactive audio files with a new approach to ear training a studentÕs progress is limited only by their willingness to practice!

A Fanatic's Guide to Ear Training and Sight Singing
Spiral Bound ISBN 1-890944-19-X   Perfect Bound ISBN 1890944-75-0

This book and CD present a method for developing good pitch recognition through sight singing. This method differs from the myriad of other sight singing books in that it develops the ability to identify and name all twelve pitches within a key center. Through this method a student gains the ability to identify sound based on it's relationship to a key and not the relationship of one note to another (i.e. interval training as commonly taught in many texts). All note groupings from one to six notes are presented giving the student a thesaurus of basic note combinations which develops sight singing and note recognition to a level unattainable before this Guide's existence.

Key Note Recognition
Spiral Bound ISBN 1-890944-30-3   Perfect Bound ISBN 1890944-77-7

This book and CD present a method for developing the ability to recognize the function of any note against a key. This method is a must for anyone who wishes to sound one note on an instrument or voice and instantly know what key a song is in. Through this method a student gains the ability to identify a sound based on its relationship to a key and not the relationship of one note to another (i.e. interval training as commonly taught in many texts). Key Center Recognition is a definite requirement before proceeding to two note ear training.

LINES Volume One: Sight Reading and Sight Singing Exercises
Spiral Bound ISBN 1-890944-09-2   Perfect Bound ISBN 1890944-76-9

This book can be used for many applications. It is an excellent source for easy half note melodies that a beginner can use to learn how to read music or for sight singing slightly chromatic lines. An intermediate or advanced student will find exercises for multi-voice reading. These exercises can also be used for multi-voice ear training. The book has the added benefit in that all exercises can be heard by downloading the audio files for each example. See http://www.muse-eek.com for details.

LINES Volume Two: Sight Reading and Sight Singing Exercises
Spiral Bound ISBN 1-594899-88-6   Perfect Bound ISBN 1594899-99-1

Recommended for those who have completed volume one, volume two introduces more complex harmonic material. This book can be used for many applications. It is an excellent source for easy quarter note melodies that a beginner can use to learn how to read music or for sight singing slightly chromatic lines. An intermediate or advanced student will find exercises for multi-voice reading. These exercises can also be used for multi-voice ear training. The book has the added benefit in that all exercises can be heard by downloading the audio files for each example. See http://www.muse-eek.com for details.

Ear Training ONE NOTE: Beginning Level
Spiral Bound ISBN 1-890944-12-2   Perfect Bound ISBN 1890944-66-1

This Book and Audio CD presents a new and exciting method for developing relative pitch ear training. It has been used with great success and is now finally available on CD. There are three levels available depending on the student's ability. This beginning level is recommended for students who have little or no music training.

Ear Training ONE NOTE: Intermediate Level
Spiral Bound ISBN 1-890944-13-0   Perfect Bound ISBN 1890944-67-X

This Audio CD and booklet presents a new and exciting method of developing relative pitch ear training. It has been used with great success and is now finally available on CD. This intermediate level is recommended for students who have had some music training but still find their skills need more development.

Ear Training ONE NOTE: Advanced Level
Spiral Bound ISBN 1-890944-14-9   Perfect Bound ISBN 1890944-68-8

This Audio CD and booklet presents a new and exciting method of developing relative pitch ear training. It has been used with great success and is now finally available on CD. There are three levels available depending on the student's ability. This advanced level is recommended for students who have worked with the intermediate level and now wish to perfect their skills.

Ear Training TWO NOTE: Beginning Level Volume One
Spiral Bound ISBN 1-890944-31-9   Perfect Bound ISBN 1890944-69-6

This Book and Audio CD continues the method of developing relative pitch ear training as set forth in the "Ear Training, One Note" series. There are six volumes in the beginning level series. Through practice, the student eventually gains the ability to recognize the key and the names of any two notes played simultaneously. Volume One concentrates on 5ths. Prerequisite: a strong grasp of the One Note method.

Ear Training TWO NOTE: Beginning Level Volume Two
Spiral Bound ISBN 1-890944-32-7   Perfect Bound ISBN 1890944-70-X

This Book and Audio CD continues the method of developing relative pitch ear training as set forth in the "Ear Training, One Note" series. There are six volumes in the beginning level series. Through practice, the student eventually gains the ability to recognize the key and the names of any two notes played simultaneously. Volume Two concentrates on 3rds. Prerequisite: a strong grasp of the One Note method.

Ear Training TWO NOTE: Beginning Level Volume Three
Spiral Bound ISBN 1-890944-33-5   Perfect Bound ISBN 1890944-71-8

This Book and Audio CD continues the method of developing relative pitch ear training as set forth in the "Ear Training, One Note" series. There are six volumes in the beginning level series. Through practice, the student eventually gains the ability to recognize the key and the names of any two notes played simultaneously. Volume Three concentrates on 6ths. Prerequisite: a strong grasp of the One Note method.

Ear Training TWO NOTE: Beginning Level Volume Four
Spiral Bound ISBN 1-890944-34-3   Perfect Bound ISBN 1890944-72-6

This Book and Audio CD continues the method of developing relative pitch ear training as set forth in the "Ear Training, One Note" series. There are six volumes in the beginning level series. Through practice, the student eventually gains the ability to recognize the key and the names of any two notes played simultaneously. Volume Four concentrates on 4ths. Prerequisite: a strong grasp of the One Note method.

Ear Training TWO NOTE: Beginning Level Volume Five
Spiral Bound ISBN 1-890944-35-1   Perfect Bound ISBN 1890944-73-4

This Book and Audio CD continues the method of developing relative pitch ear training as set forth in the "Ear Training, One Note" series. There are six volumes in the beginning level series. Through practice, the student eventually gains the ability to recognize the key and the names of any two notes played simultaneously. Volume Five concentrates on 2nds. Prerequisite: a strong grasp of the One Note method.

Ear Training TWO NOTE: Beginning Level Volume Six
Spiral Bound ISBN 1-890944-36-X   Perfect Bound ISBN 1890944-74-2

This Book and Audio CD continues the method of developing relative pitch ear training as set forth in the "Ear Training, One Note" series. There are six volumes in the beginning level series. Through practice, the student eventually gains the ability to recognize the key and the names of any two notes played simultaneously. Volume Six concentrates on 7ths. Prerequisite: a strong grasp of the One Note method.

Comping Styles Series

This series is built on the progressions found in Chord Workbook Volume One. Each book covers a specific style of music and presents exercises to help a guitarist, bassist or drummer master that style. Audio CDs are also available so a student can play along with each example and really get "into the groove."

Comping Styles for the Guitar Volume Two FUNK
Spiral Bound ISBN 1-890944-07-6   Perfect Bound ISBN 1890944-60-2

This volume teaches a student how to play guitar or piano in a funk style. 36 Progressions are presented: 12 keys of a Major and Minor Blues plus 12 keys of Rhythm Changes A different groove is presented for each exercise giving the student a wide range of funk rhythms to master. An Audio CD is also included so a student can play along with each example and really get "into the groove." The audio CD contains "trio" versions of each exercise with Guitar, Bass and Drums.

Comping Styles for the Bass Volume Two FUNK
Spiral Bound ISBN 1-890944-08-4   Perfect Bound ISBN 1890944-61-0

This volume teaches a student how to play bass in a funk style. 36 Progressions are presented: 12 keys of a Major and Minor Blues plus 12 keys of Rhythm Changes A different groove is presented for each exercise giving the student a wide range of funk rhythms to master. An Audio CD is also included so a student can play along with each example and really get "into the groove." The audio CD contains "trio" versions of each exercise with Guitar, Bass and Drums.

Jazz and Blues Bass Line
Spiral Bound ISBN 1-890944-15-7   Perfect Bound ISBN 1890944-16-5

This book covers the basics of bass line construction. A theoretical guide to building bass lines is presented along with 36 chord progressions utilizing the twelve keys of a Major and Minor Blues, plus twelve keys of Rhythm Changes. A reharmonization section is also provided which demonstrates how to reharmonize a chord progression on the spot.

Time Series

The Doing Time series presents a method for contacting, developing and relying on your internal time sense: This series is an excellent resource for any musician who is serious about developing strong internal sense of time. This is particularly useful in any kind of music where the rhythms and time signatures may be very complex or free, and there is no conductor.

THE BIG METRONOME
Spiral Bound ISBN 1-890944-37-8   Perfect Bound ISBN 1890944-82-3

The Big Metronome is designed to help you develop a better internal sense of time. This is accomplished by requiring you to "feel time" rather than having you rely on the steady click of a metronome. The idea is to slowly wean yourself away from an external device and rely on your internal/natural sense of time. The exercises presented work in conjunction with the three CDs that accompany this book. CD 1 presents the first 13 settings from a traditional metronome 40-66; the second CD contains metronome markings 69-116, and the third CD contains metronome markings 120-208. The first CD gives you a 2 bar count off and a click every measure, the second CD gives you a 2 bar count off and a click every 2 measures, the 3rd CD gives you a 2 bar count off and a click every 4 measures. By presenting all common metronome markings a student can use these 3 CDs as a replacement for a traditional metronome.

Doing Time with the Blues Volume One
Spiral Bound ISBN 1-890944-17-3   Perfect Bound ISBN 1890944-78-5

The book and CD presents a method for gaining an internal sense of time thereby eliminating dependence on a metronome. The book presents the basic concept for developing good time and also includes exercises that can be practiced with the CD. The CD provides eight 8 minute tracks at different tempos in which the time is delineated every 2 bars, and with an extra hit every 12 bars to outline the blues form. The student may then use the exercises presented in the book to gain control of their execution or improvise to gain control of their ideas using this bare minimum of time delineation.

Doing Time with the Blues Volume Two
Spiral Bound ISBN 1-890944-18-1   Perfect Bound ISBN 1890944-79-3

This is the 2nd volume of a four volume series which presents a method for developing a musicians internal sense of time, thereby eliminating dependence on a metronome. This 2nd volume presents different exercises which further the development of this time sense. This 2nd volume begins to test even a professional level players ability. The CD provides eight 8 minute tracks at different tempos in which the time is delineated every 4 bars with an extra hit every 12 bars to outline the blues form. New exercises are also included that can be practiced with the CD. This series is an excellent resource for any musician who is serious about developing an internal sense of time.

Doing Time with 32 Bars Volume One
Spiral Bound ISBN 1-890944-22-X   Spiral Bound ISBN 1890944-80-7

The book and CD presents a method for gaining an internal sense of time thereby eliminating dependence on a metronome. The book presents the basic concept for developing good time and also includes exercises that can be practiced with the CD. The CD provides eight 8 minute tracks at different tempos in which the time is delineated every 2 bars, with an extra hit every 32 to outline the 32 bar form. The student may then use the exercises presented in the book to gain control of their execution or improvise to gain control of their ideas using this bare minimum of time delineation.

Doing Time with 32 Bars Volume Two
Spiral Bound ISBN 1-890944-23-8   Spiral Bound ISBN 1890944-81-5

This is the 2nd volume of a four volume series which presents a method for developing a musicians internal sense of time, thereby eliminating dependence on a metronome.. This 2nd volume presents different exercises which further the development of this time sense. This 2nd volume begins to test even a professional level players ability. The CD provides eight 8 minute tracks at different tempos in which the time is delineated every 4 bars with an extra hit every 32 bars to outline the 32 bar form. New exercises are also included that can be practiced with the CD. This series is an excellent resource for any musician who is serious about developing an internal sense of time.

Time Transformation
Spiral Bound ISBN 1594899-929-0   Perfect Bound ISBN 1594899-930-4

"Time Transformation" is designed to take the application of odd meters to another level of mastery. Etudes are presented in 12 keys using the time signatures of 3/4, 4/4, 5/4, 6/4 and 7/4. There are a total of 60 highly syncopated studies that are presented using various combinations of eighth note and sixteenth note rhythms. Book also includes downloadable "vamps" that can be used in various ways with each étude.

Other Workbooks

Music Theory Workbook for All Instruments, Volume 1: Interval and Chord Construction
Spiral Bound ISBN 1594899-51-7   Perfect Bound ISBN 1890944-46-7

This book provides real hands-on application of intervals and chords. A theory section written in concise and easy to understand language prepares the student for all exercises. Worksheets are given that quiz a student about intervals and chord construction using staff notation. Answers are supplied in the back of the book enabling a student to work without a teacher.

Jazz Piano Vocabulary by Roberta Piket, Volume 1: The Major Scale
Spiral Bound ISBN 1594899-51-7   Perfect Bound ISBN 1594899-51-7

This is the 1st volume in a series designed to help the student of jazz piano learn and apply jazz scales by mastering each scale and its uses in improvisation. Each book focuses on a different scale, illustrating the scale in all twelve keys with complete fingerings. Also provided are chords and left hand voicings to match, exercises and études to apply the material to improvising, ideas for further study and listening, and detailed suggestions on how to prace the material. Volume 1 also includes a detailed primer in note reading, basic theory, and rhythmic notation.

Jazz Piano Vocabulary by Roberta Piket, Volume 2: The Dorian Mode
Spiral Bound ISBN 1890944-96-3   Perfect Bound ISBN 1890944-98-X

The 2nd volume in the series, this book focuses on the Dorian scale and applies it to improvising on minor seventh chords. The Dorian scale is presented in all twelve keys with complete fingerings. The book also contains left hand voicings, exercises, many examples, an étude to help apply the material, ideas for further study, an extended discography, and detailed instruction and practice tips.

Jazz Piano Vocabulary by Roberta Piket, Volume 3: The Phrygian Mode
Spiral Bound ISBN 1594899-53-3   Perfect Bound ISBN 1594899-54-1

For students who have covered the basics in Volume 1,2 and 5, this book focuses in the Phrygian and Spanish Phrygian scales. It discusess "modern" jazz chords such as the "Phrygian" chord (susb9). The scale is presented in all 12 keys with fingerings. It also provides a detailed treatise on a modal approach to chord voicings, practice tips and a Phrygian étude.

Jazz Piano Vocabulary by Roberta Piket, Volume 4: The Lydian Mode
Spiral Bound ISBN 1594899-55-X   Perfect Bound ISBN 1594899-56-8

Volume 4 features the Lydian scale in all twelve keys; two octaves up and down with complete piano fingerings. Chords are presented with left hand voicings that work with the scale (along with fingerings) Also included are exercises to develop the concept of melodic phrasing in improvisation, examples of the use of the Lydian scale in the jazz repertoire, and detailed instructions on how to practice the material. Added feature: author can be contacted online if questions arise.

Jazz Piano Vocabulary by Roberta Piket, Volume 5: The Mixolydian Mode
Spiral Bound ISBN 1594899-57-6   Perfect Bound ISBN 1594899-58-4

This book focuses on the Mixolydian scale and applies it to improvising on dominant seventh and dominant seventh sus chords. The scale is presented in all twelve keys with fingerings. The book also contains an introduction to approach notes, an explanation and étude on twelve bar blues form, left hand voicings, exercises, melodic examples, instruction and practice tips.

Guitar Method Series

This series of books distills several of our previous publications into a method currently in use at New York University for the Summer Guitar Intensive Program. Content is geared towards any musician that is looking to expand their understanding of typical musical concepts but also covers many musically uncharted territories. Material concentrates on essential information the student must master in order to become a professional guitarist in the heavily competitive New York City music scene. This series of books starts with the most basic beginning guitar information and takes the reader to the most advanced musical concepts.

New York Guitar Method Primer Book 1
Spiral Bound ISBN 159489-911-8   Perfect Bound ISBN 159489-912-6

This book provides students with an excellent foundation in theory, ear training, chord and scale comprehension on the guitar. It is a prerequisite for entering New York University's Summer Guitar Intensive Program and provides students studying independently with the tools they will need to successfully move on to Primer Book 2.

New York Guitar Method Primer Book 2
Spiral Bound ISBN 159489-915-0   Perfect Bound ISBN 159489-916-9

This book provides students with an excellent foundation in theory, ear training, chord and scale comprehension on the guitar. It is a prerequisite for entering New York University's Summer Guitar Intensive Program and provides students studying independently with the tools they will need to successfully move on to New York Guitar Method Book 1. "New York Guitar Method Primer Ensemble Book Two" is the companion book for "New York Guitar Method Primer Book Two." This book contains music examples of the information covered in this book so that a student can apply the information through memorization and sight reading.

New York Guitar Method Primer Ensemble Book 2
Spiral Bound ISBN 159489-913-4   Perfect Bound ISBN 159489-914-2

This book is a prerequisite for entering New York University's Summer Guitar Intensive Program and provides students studying independently with the tools they will need to successfully move on to Volume 1. Our Ensemble Method presents a breakthrough approach for teaching guitarist how to sightread. Each chapter has eighth note, sixteenth note, single string, lines, and chord exercises. The book also includes modal jazz vamps and solos and is an excellent resource for lab/ensemble studies as it contains 3 and 4-part reading examples.

New York Guitar Method Volume 1
Spiral Bound ISBN 159489-987-8   Perfect Bound ISBN 159489-900-2

This book contains 22 scales and their theory which are covered in great detail. Multiple types of chord voicings along with an in-Depth coverage of articulations. The application of scales through modal sequences is also explained. The following musical concepts are covered: Finding the Right Scale for Any Chord, Finding the Natural Scale Sound, Thinking the Way You Hear, Two to Eleven Note Scale Possibilities along with a list of 2,048 Scale Possibilities which contain the root. Slash Chords, Regular Chords and Slash Chords, Slash Chord Possibilities, Reharmonization Theory, Adding Tensions.
    "New York Guitar Method Ensemble Book One" is the companion book for "New York Guitar Method Volume One." This book contains music examples of the information covered in this book so that a student can apply the information through memorization and sight reading.

New York Guitar Method Ensemble Book 1
Spiral Bound ISBN 159489-905-3   Perfect Bound ISBN 159489-906-1

Volume One focuses on reading jazz solos that demonstrate the many uses of scales as discussed in the accompanying New York Guitar Method Volume 1. The book also includes jazz and classical reading études and is an excellent resource for lab/ensemble studies as it contains 3 and 4-part reading examples.

New York Guitar Method Volume 2
Spiral Bound ISBN 159489-901-0   Perfect Bound ISBN 159489-902-9

This is the second book in our series currently in use at New York University for the Summer Guitar Intensive Program. A continuation of Volume 1, Volume 2 focuses on approach notes and discusses how to apply approaches to jazz lines in order to create the signature sounding lines of bebop through the contemporary sounding lines of the modern masters. "New York Guitar Method Ensemble Book Two" is the companion book for "New York Guitar Method Volume Two." This book contains music examples of the information covered in this book so that a student can apply the information through memorization and sight reading.

New York Guitar Method Ensemble Book 2
Spiral Bound ISBN 159489-907-X   Perfect Bound ISBN 159489-908-8

Volume Two focuses on reading jazz solos that demonstrate the many uses of approach notes as discussed in the accompanying New York Guitar Method Volume 2. The book also includes jazz and classical reading études and is an excellent resource for lab/ensemble studies as it contains 3 and 4-part reading examples.

Set Theory Method

This series of books explores the relationships of post tonal theory to contemporary improvisation. It is meant to bridge the gap between jazz theory and contemporary set theory.

Sonic Resource Guide
Spiral Bound ISBN 159489-933-9   Perfect Bound ISBN 159489-934-7

"Set Theory for Improvisation" examines the use and organization of pitch class sets for improvisation and composition. Two through twelve note pitch class sets are explored and their application to the harmony and melody shown through multiple examples. The companion series "Set Theory for Improvisation Ensemble" is recommended as both a overall musical development tool and as a sight reading gold mine. For all instruments.

Set Theory for Improvisation Ensemble Method

The ensemble method gives examples of applying post tonal theory to contemporary improvisation in the form of études. Each étude explores the melodic possibilities using various combinations of note groupings, rhythms, metric level, melodic range and density. There are 12 études in each book, one in each key which can be played over a variety of chords. These études range from highly diatonic to non-diatonic examples depending on the organization of the material. For all instruments.

Set Theory for Improvisation Ensemble Method: Hexatonic 027 027
Spiral Bound ISBN 159489-920-7   Perfect Bound ISBN 159489-921-5

Set Theory for Improvisation Ensemble Method: Hexatonic 027 016
Spiral Bound ISBN 159489-922-3   Perfect Bound ISBN 159489-923-1

Set Theory for Improvisation Ensemble Method: Hexatonic 027 026
Spiral Bound ISBN 159489-924-X   Perfect Bound ISBN 159489-925-8

E-Books

The Bruce Arnold series of instructional E-books is for the student who wishes to target specific areas of study that are of particular interest. Many of these books are excerpted from other larger texts. The excerpted source is listed for each book. These books are available on-line at www.muse-eek.com as well as at many e-tailers throughout the internet. These books can also be purchased in the traditional book binding format. (See the ISBN number for proper format)

Chord Velocity: Volume One, Learning to switch between chords quickly
E-book ISBN 1-890944-88-2   Traditional Book Binding ISBN 1-890944-97-1

The first hurdle a beginning guitarist encounters is difficulty in switching between chords quickly enough to make a chord progression sound like music. This book provides exercises that help a student gradually increase the speed with which they change chords. Special free audio files are also available on the muse-eek.com website to make practice more productive and fun. Within a few weeks, remarkable improvement can be achieved using this method. This book is excerpted from "1st Steps for a Beginning Guitarist Volume One."

Guitar Technique: Volume One, Learning the basics to fast, clean, accurate and fluid performance skills.
E-book ISBN 1-890944-91-2   Traditional Book Binding ISBN 1-890944-99-8

This book is for both the beginning guitarist or the more experienced guitarist who wishes to improve their technique. All aspects of the physical act of playing the guitar are covered, from how to hold a guitar to the specific way each hand is involved in the playing process. Pictures and videos are provided to help clarify each technique. These pictures and videos are either contained in the book or can be downloaded at www.muse-eek.com This book is excerpted from "1st Steps for a Beginning Guitarist Volume One."

Accompaniment: Volume One, Learning to Play Bass and Chords Simultaneously
E-book ISBN 1-890944-87-4   Traditional Book Binding ISBN 1-890944-96-3

The techniques found within this book are an excellent resource for creating and understanding how to play bass and chords simultaneously in a jazz or blues style. Special attention is paid to understanding how this technique is created, thereby enabling the student to recreate this style with other pieces of music. This book is excerpted from the book "Guitar Clinic."

Beginning Rhythm Studies: Volume One, Learning the basics of reading rhythm and playing in time.
E-book ISBN 1-890944-89-0   Traditional Book Binding 1-890944-98-X

This book covers the basics for anyone wishing to understand or improve their rhythmic abilities. Simple language is used to show the student how to read and play rhythm. Exercises are presented which can accelerate the learning process. Audio examples in the form of midifiles are available on the muse-eek.com website to facilitate learning the correct rhythm in time. This book is excerpted from the book "Rhythm Primer."

www.ingramcontent.com/pod-product-compliance
Lightning Source LLC
LaVergne TN
LVHW061319060426
835507LV00019B/2221